CPSIA information can be obtained
at www.ICGtesting.com
Printed in the USA
LVHW022018080519
617104LV00015B/988/P

9 781092 240994